BOOK ANALYSIS

Written by Marie Bouhon
Translated by Jessica Foster

AF131409

One Hundred Years of Solitude

BY GABRIEL GARCÍA MÁRQUEZ

Bright
≡Summaries.com

**Shed new light
on your favorite books with**

Bright
≡Summaries.com

www.brightsummaries.com

GABRIEL GARCÍA MÁRQUEZ

COLOMBIAN WRITER AND JOURNALIST

- **Born in Aracataca (Colombia) in 1927**
- **Died in Mexico City in 2014**
- **Notable works:**
  - *The Leaf Storm* (1955), novel
  - *Chronicle of a Death Foretold* (1981), novel
  - *Love in the Time of Cholera* (1985)

Considered by French newspaper *Le Monde* as "one of the greatest writers of the 20th century", Gabriel García Márquez brought international renown to Latin American literature and, in particular, authors from the 'Latin American boom', such as Jorge Luis Borges (Argentinian, 1899-1986), Julio Córtazar (Argentinian, 1914-1984) and Mario Vargas Llosa (Peruvian, born in 1936).

Although he was not behind the genre of magic realism, his novel *One Hundred Years of Solitude* is one of its most notable examples. Themes such as solitude, death, violence and power are omnipresent in the work of this talented writer, who won the Nobel Prize in Literature in 1982.

ONE HUNDRED YEARS OF SOLITUDE

A MAJOR WORK ON THE LATIN AMERICAN LANDSCAPE

- **Genre:** magic realism
- **Reference edition**: García Márquez, G. (2000) *One Hundred Years of Solitude*. Trans. Rabassa, G. London: Penguin.
- **First edition:** 1967
- **Themes:** solitude, time, death, family, violence, misfortune, generations.

First published in Argentina in 1967, *One Hundred Years of Solitude* is considered by the Chilean poet Pablo Neruda (1904-1973) as "the greatest revelation in the Spanish language since Don Quixote [a novel written by Miguel de Cervantes in the 18th century]". The novel was written in absolute poverty and destitution – the writer had to sell some of his belongings in order to be able to send the manuscript to an editor – yet was so successful that it brought Gabriel García Márquez international renown. Now translated into almost 35 languages, it has sold more than 30 million copies and was awarded both the French *Prix du Meilleure Livre Étranger* (Best Foreign Book Prize) in 1969 and the Venezuelan Rómulo Gallegos prize in 1972.

Through themes such as solitude and oblivion, the novel tells two stories: that of a family over seven generations, and that of the village that they founded, from its construction to its fall.

SUMMARY

A COMPLEX FAMILY TREE

José Arcadio Buendia and Ursula Iguarán are an emblematic couple, behind the six Buendia generations and the village of Macondo. Despite their fears that, according to legend, an incestuous couple would bear a child with a pig's tail, the two cousins decide to start a family. When their children are born, they are relieved to see that neither José Arcadio, nor Aureliano nor Amaranta are deformed. Their family continues to grow when they adopt Rebecca, an Indian orphan, and Arcadio, the son of José Arcadio and Pilar Ternera. They decide to raise them as their own children: Arcadio never discovers that the people who raised him are actually his grandparents.

Then the second generation flies the nest: Aureliano has a child with Pilar, who is called Aureliano José, but also has 17 others during the war, all to different mothers and all named after him. José Arcadio, who has just returned from a journey with a group of travellers, falls for his adoptive sister Rebecca and decides to marry her. Amaranta, on the other hand, remains a spinster, although she does have a special relationship with her nephew, Aureliano José.

In the third generation, although Arcadio is the only one to have children (Remedios, José Arcadio II and Aureliano II), he does not raise them, as he dies when they are still very young. Aureliano II is also the only one to have children: Amaranta Ursula, José Arcadio and Renata Remedios.

Renata, his youngest, has intimate relations with Mauricio Babilonia when they are not married, and is therefore sent to a convent where she gives birth to their son, Aureliano Babilonia.

The parenthood of this child is kept secret and it is therefore unknowingly that he falls in love with his aunt, Amaranta Ursula. From this incestuous relationship, Aureliano, the last of the Buendias, is born, cursed with a pig's tail, just as the legend predicted. His mother dies in childbirth and his father, overcome with grief, forgets about the child, thus causing the infant's death. Aureliano Babilonia then isolates himself completely from the outside world and sets to work translating the manuscripts of the traveller Melquíades.

Buendia family tree

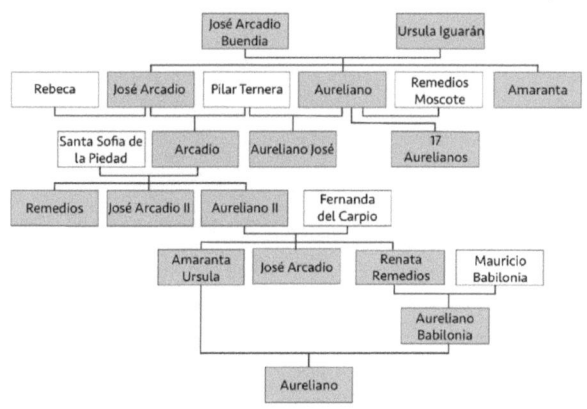

THE STORY OF A VILLAGE

Following a fight in which José Arcadio Buendia kills his enemy Prudencio Aguilar, he decides to leave his village, as he is haunted by the ghost of his victim. Under the pretext of an expedition to find the ocean and build a new town there, he leaves, with several other families. After months of searching in vain, they settle in a place which will become the village of Macondo.

Initially, this small village is self-sufficient, completely isolated from the outside world, but gradually travellers start to go there, bringing the most recent inventions – notably mirrors and flying carpets – and the country's news. Thus begins the expansion of Macondo, of which the first stage is the arrival of the first foreign family, the Moscotes. Don Apolinar Moscote wants to run the small town in accordance with the conservative government, and instigates the first political conflicts: the inhabitants then divide into two groups, liberals and conservatives. Aureliano Buendia then leads a rebellion which will cause a civil war in which both factions are opposed throughout the country.

Macondo, thanks to the development of its trade, small businesses and means of communication, becomes a significant modern town in the region. However, the first signs of decline begin to show. Firstly, following a strike on a banana plantation, all the workers are killed by the national army. Then there are the torrential rains, which plague Macondo for almost five years, isolating it again from the rest of the world and causing the exile of many inhabitants. The town, in the same way as the Buendia family, gradually falls into oblivion and solitude. Intense winds destroy the last signs of life in the village, leaving nothing behind them.

THE MISFORTUNE OF THE BUENDIA FAMILY

Melquíades, the leader of a group of travellers, goes to Macondo every spring, before the village's expansion period. Early on, José Arcadio Buendia befriends this mysterious man who brings him hundreds of miraculous things. After his death and resurrection, Melquíades is welcomed by the Buendias, and begins writing manuscripts that nobody can decipher. This is in fact the inscription of the curse that condemns the family to one hundred years of solitude, oblivion and collapse.

The first signs of this curse appear just after the arrival of Rebecca in Macondo. These are the plague of insomnia and the plague of oblivion. From then onwards, the inhabitants affected by these evils no longer sleep and forget everything, including their past and the names of simple objects. But a potion provided by Melquíades cures these illnesses. Unfortunately, the solution is only temporary and the condemnation will take more radical forms as time passes: the solitude and isolation of the Buendia family, whom nobody remembers; the torrential rains and the winds that destroy Macondo. Only Aureliano Babilonia, the last survivor of his family, manages to decipher these manuscripts. However, as he reads, he realises that he cannot stop reading as, when he finishes the last lines, both the village and himself will be destroyed.

CHARACTER STUDY

The novel tells the story of an entire family and of a village through several generations. There are easily more than 30 characters, therefore the selection below only features the most important, those whose actions have a profound influence on the plot.

JOSÉ ARCADIO BUENDIA

José Arcadio Buendia is the instigator of a journey that leads several families to build the village of Macondo. He suggests this journey in order to escape the ghost of his enemy that he killed, Prudencio Aguilar. His strategy works as he then does not see the ghost for several years.

José Arcadio Buendia is a leader, who maintains order in the village thanks to his natural authority and his sense of fairness. He has a curious nature and he always looks forward to the arrival of the travellers, who bring miraculous things. As he too wishes to understand how modern objects and various phenomena work, he does many experiments and entertains himself in his laboratory, dismantling various things. He also introduces his son, Aureliano, to alchemy.

Gradually, due to the return of Prudencio's ghost, he goes insane and loses touch with reality. His family tie him to the trunk of a chestnut tree, with which his body becomes one. In complete harmony with nature, he talks to his old enemy. A few days before his death, his wife takes him back to his bedroom, so that he can die with dignity.

URSULA IGUARÁN

Ursula Iguarán, along with her cousin José Arcadio Buendia, forms half of the founding couple of Macondo. She is highly superstitious and fears that her children will be born deformed by a pig's tail or resembling iguanas due to her incestuous relationship. Despite this, she is the source of a family of seven generations and knows nearly all of her descendants. She lives for over 100 years, and turns out to be the real head of the family. Moreover, she looks after the house, raises the children and grandchildren and maintains order in the village when her husband is busy with his inventions.

To meet the needs of her household, she runs a successful baking business, which allows the Buendias to live in modern comfort. She is also a healer in her spare time, and treats the various ills and illnesses with plant-based potions, which she makes for the occasion.

MELQUIADES

Melquíades is the head of a group of travellers who regularly visit Macondo. Fairly early on, he establishes a close friendship with José Arcadio Buendia. As they share the same curiosity for the things of the world, they both undertake many experiments, including the creation of gold from other metals or photographing God using daguerreotype; unfortunately these all fail.

One day, the Buendia family notices that Melquíades, sadly, is not with the other travellers who arrive for spring. He has in fact died of a fever in the seas of Asia. A few years later, however, he comes back to life and knocks on the door of his friend, who welcomes him with open arms, without asking questions. They then continue their experiments, but gradually Melquíades becomes isolated and starts scribbling on old parchment. Upon his second death, many people try in vain to decipher his writings, but only Aureliano Babilonia eventually succeeds.

JOSÉ ARCADIO

José Arcadio is the oldest son of José Arcadio Buendia and Ursula Iguarán. He is a quiet child and is not particularly interested in his father's experiments. During his adolescence, he falls in love with Pilar Ternera, the maid. After every night he spends with her, he tells his brother Aureliano everything, which brings them closer. One day in spring, Pilar announces that she is pregnant. The future father, frightened, leaves her to distract himself with the travellers. He then meets a girl with whom he falls in love and leaves the village with the nomadic group.

Years later, when he returns, he has tattoos, is muscular, has forgotten all his manners and has a strong character. He meets Rebecca again, his adoptive sister, who has grown up to be much more beautiful. They isolate themselves from the family in order to pursue a romantic relationship without having to hide, despite their mother's forbidding it. Once he has moved into a small house with his wife, José Arcadio seizes the neighbouring land and starts collecting taxes. He also gets closer to Arcadio, the son he had with

Pilar, without ever admitting to him how they are related.

AURELIANO BUENDIA, OR THE COLONEL

Aureliano is the second son of the founding couple of the village of Macondo. He is a mystical character who turns out to be a prophesier. Indeed, from his birth, he is very sharp and predicts several events with great certainty, such as a saucepan falling or a stranger arriving. Later, he even announces the date of his father's death and foils several of his plots due to his premonitions. He also takes interest in his father's experiments and becomes a specialist in making small golden fish, which he gives out to everyone.

Having never been in love, he falls for the young Remedios Moscote, who is only nine years old at the time. Eventually he convinces both his and her parents to accept their marriage, which happens once Remedios reaches puberty. Unfortunately, the young girl dies in childbirth, along with the child.

Aureliano is inconsolable in the face of this loss. A short while later, his father-in-law introduces him to politics. After discovering the fraudulent nature of the vote, he joins the liberals and leads a rebellion. He shows his value in the war by leading a group of rebels and winning several battles, and is named the Colonel. He is determined, and refuses to surrender on many occasions, even when all hope seems lost. Eventually, however, he signs a peace treaty with the conservative government, then tries to commit suicide, but fails. He isolates himself from the village and spends the rest of his days in his workshop, alone, crafting small fish.

THE MEN OF THE BUENDIA FAMILY

Among the men of the Buendia family, we can identify two types of character: those who are like José Arcadio and those who are more similar to the character of Aureliano.

The first type have an impulsive character and are solidly built, while the second type are rather quiet and anti-social. Their first names give an insight into their character as those who belong to the first group have names derived from that of José Arcadio (Arcadio, José Arcadio II, José Arcadio) while the names of the others are derived from that of Aureliano (Aureliano José, Aureliano II, Aureliano Babilonia).

ANALYSIS

MAGIC REALISM

One Hundred Years of Solitude is a novel belonging to the genre of magic realism. Although the term first appeared in 1925 in an essay by Franz Roh (German historian, photographer and art critic, 1890-1965), describing expressionist works of art, this genre officially spread in Latin American literature during the 1940s. The main authors who used it, other than Gabriel García Márquez, were Jorge Luis Borges, Miguel Ángel Asturias (Guatemalan, 1899-1974), Alejo Carpentier (French, 1904-1980) and Juan Rolfo (Mexican, 1917-1986). Thus, *One Hundred Years of Solitude* is far from being the instigator of this movement; it is, however, the most cited example of the genre, and it is thanks to this work that the trend became known globally.

As its name suggests, magic realism mixes an element of realism with a supernatural dimension. Thus, the setting of the story is completely believable: places can be linked to existing locations and the events described could have really happened. Certain elements, however, come from the realms of the imaginary, magic and fantasy.

García Márquez's novel mixes these two dimensions very effectively. On the one hand, the story takes place in a small, isolated village, which strongly resembles Aracataca, the writer's hometown. The pervasive armed conflict between the liberals and the conservatives, in reality, recalls the Thousand Days' War, a civil war that took place in Colombia between 17 October 1899 and 21 November 1902. The workers' strike on the banana plantation and the massacre that follows are a direct reference to the revolt, in November 1928, of the workers of the United Fruit Company. As well as the different elements that define the credible spatio-temporal framework of the story, the inventions that the writer mentions are also contemporary: the telegraph, the daguerreotype, the train, and so forth.

On the other hand, the work is peppered with supernatural elements such as the village priest's levitation when he drinks hot chocolate, the transformation of a traveller into a puddle of tar, the flying carpet, the rain of flowers when José Arcadio Buendia dies, or the presence of ghosts. It is worth noting that these elements, although they do not exist in our reality, are present in the story's reality, which is why they do not particularly shock the narrator or the various characters. This novel thus shows us a world in which reality and magic coexist naturally.

CYCLICAL TIME

The temporality of this novel is unusual and can perhaps be described as cyclic. Indeed, events often repeat themselves, much like the names and characteristics of the various characters, in such a way that the reader is under the impression that the story never progresses, as if it is stuck in an endless loop. The most significant example of this is the presence of incest in relationships between the Buendia family members, which recurs from generation to generation: it begins with José Arcadio Buendia and Ursula Iguarán, the two cousins, continues with Amaranta and Arcadio, her nephew, and concludes with the relationship between Aureliano Babilonia and Amaranta Ursula, his aunt.

Moreover, every twist in the novel is, in fact, an integral part of Melquíades' manuscripts, which the reader only discovers at the end of the novel. Everything was written, predetermined and inevitable. This double dimension of the story, through the manuscript read by Aureliano Babilonia, is in fact a 'mise en abyme'.

GOOD TO KNOW

'Mise en abyme' is a process that consists of presenting an element within another element of the same kind. We often find it in paintings when, for example, the subjects of a picture also appear in the background, in a mirror (such as in *The Arnolfini Portrait* (1434) by Jan Van Eyck – Flemish painter, around 1390-1441). In literature, it is shown through the presence of a subplot that resembles the main plot, for example when a character reads a book which tells the exact story of the work that the actual reader is reading. This process is notably used in *Don Quixote* (1605 then 1615) by Miguel de Cervantes (Spanish writer, 1547-1616), in *The Neverending Story* (1979) by Michael Ende (German writer, 1929-1995) or even in *The Truth about the Harry Quebert Affair* (2012) by Joël Dicker (Swiss French writer, born in 1985).

THE THEME OF SOLITUDE

Solitude is present throughout the novel, appearing in certain characters, the location of the village or even through death. As well as the book's title, the 100 years of solitude correspond to the Buendia family curse: these people, condemned to a life of solitude, create a village that is totally isolated from the world. Despite technological advances (roads, the telegraph, and so on), Macondo remains a rather inconvenient port of call. It is only with the advent of the train that the town really becomes accessible to the rest of the country, but this will not be advantageous: terrible events then unfold, from the massacre of the workers to the torrential rains and winds that destroy the small town.

On top of this, most of the characters embody a form of solitude: José Arcadio Buendia, the founder, trapped in his own delirium, is tied to a tree, where he lives alone, away from the world and from reality; Ursula is trapped in her home, as she becomes blind; the Colonel Aureliano is alone in his laboratory making little gold fish; Amaranta rejects all the romantic proposals that she receives; Rebecca, when José Arcadio dies, isolates herself and no longer sees anyone, except for one servant; Aureliano Babilonia stays in Macondo where everyone has forgotten him and where he finishes deciphering the manuscripts alone in a small room.

The sense of solitude heightens at the end of the novel, through the oblivion that all the inhabitants of Macondo experience during the plague of oblivion, then through that of the country who no longer remember the existence of the village and, finally, through the experience of the Buendias when, despite their invitations, nobody comes to their parties. This causes the isolation not just of the town in the face of the rest of the world, but also of the characters between themselves and of certain protagonists towards reality.

FURTHER REFLECTION

SOME QUESTIONS TO THINK ABOUT...

- What justifies *One Hundred Years of Solitude*'s place in the genre of magic realism? Use five examples from the novel.
- The characters in the book are afraid of having children born with pig's tails. Why are they afraid of this? In your opinion, which elements led to the birth of the last Buendia with that very feature?
- Explain the title of the book, drawing examples from the text.
- In your opinion, how does the magical dimension present in the book not appear supernatural? Explain your answer using examples from the book.
- Explain and give examples of both the declines that we see in *One Hundred Years of Solitude*: that of the family and that of the village.
- Which elements give the story its cyclical nature?
- Who do you think are the most important characters in the novel? Explain your answer.
- Comment on the following extract:

> "There was no mystery in the heart of a Buendía that was impenetrable for her because a century of cards and experience had taught her that the history of the family was a machine with unavoidable repetitions, a turning wheel that would have gone on spilling into eternity were it not for the progressive and irremediable wearing of the axle" (p.288).

- Although the book is internationally acclaimed, it has never been adapted for film. What do you think could be the reason for this?
- Compare *One Hundred Years of Solitude* with the novel *Pedro Paramo* (1955) by Juan Rolfo, which also belongs to the magic realism genre. What are the similarities and differences?

We want to hear from you!
Leave a comment on your online library
and share your favourite books on social media!

FURTHER READING

REFERENCE EDITION

- García Márquez, G. (2000) *One Hundred Years of Solitude.* Trans. Rabassa, G. London: Penguin.

REFERENCE STUDIES

- Chao, R., Delcas, M. and Noiville, F. (2014) Mort de Gabriel García Márquez, légende de la littérature. *Le Monde.* [Online]. [Accessed 20 November 2015]. Available from: <http://www.lemonde.fr/disparitions/article/2014/04/17/l-ecrivain-gabriel-garcia-marquez-est-mort_4401388_3382.html>
- Fauchier, J. (2006) L'amnésie chez G. García Márquez. De la disparition physique des peuples à la disparition de la mémoire collective. *Babel: littératures plurielles.* Vol. 13, p. 121-139.
- Martin G. (2009) *Gabriel García Marquez : une vie.* Paris: Grasset.
- Ordine N. (2012) *Les portraits de Gabriel García Márquez : la répétition et la différence.* Paris: Belles Lettres.

Bright ≡Summaries.com

More guides to rediscover your love of literature

Animal Farm
BY GEORGE ORWELL

The Stranger
BY ALBERT CAMUS

Harry Potter and the Sorcerer's Stone
BY J.K. ROWLING

The Silence of the Sea
BY VERCORS

Antigone
BY JEAN ANOUILH

The Flowers of Evil
BY BAUDELAIRE

www.brightsummaries.com

©BrightSummaries.com, 2016. All rights reserved.

www.brightsummaries.com

Ebook EAN: 9782806279620

Paperback EAN: 9782806284174

Legal Deposit: D/2016/12603/363

Cover: © Primento

Digital conception by Primento, the digital partner of publishers.